Beverly's Garden

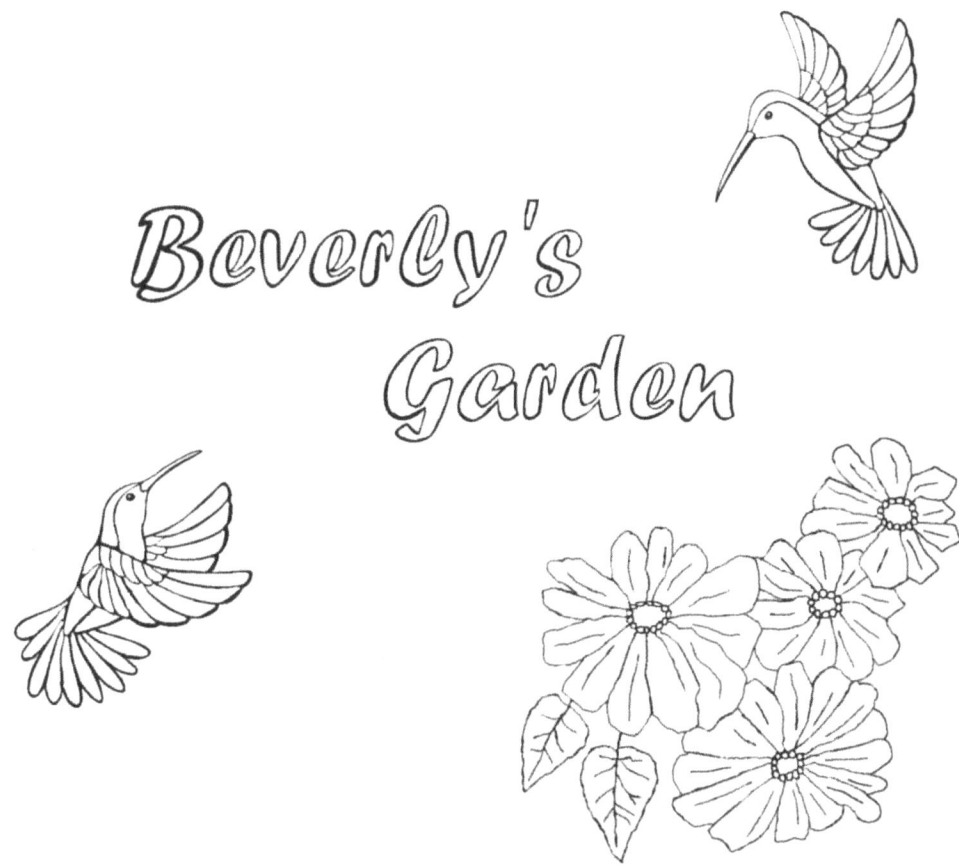

Everything that slows us down and forces patience, everything that sets us back into the slow circles of nature is a help. Gardening is an instrument of grace. -May Sarton

Beverly's Garden
Adult Coloring Book
Line Art by Vicki Dinnel
Copyright 2021 All Rights Reserved

ISBN 9798720706937
Independently published

This book belongs to:

_____

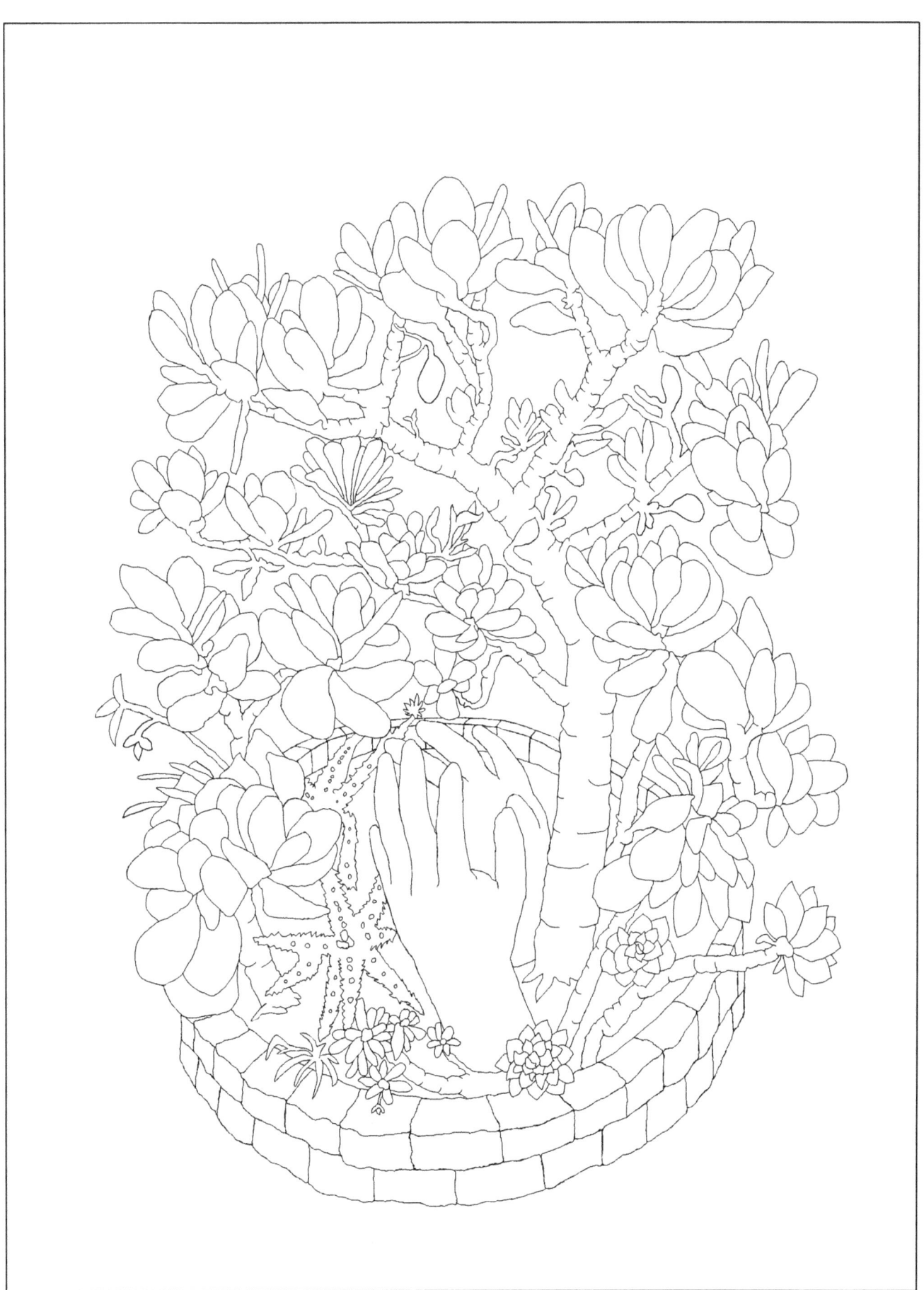

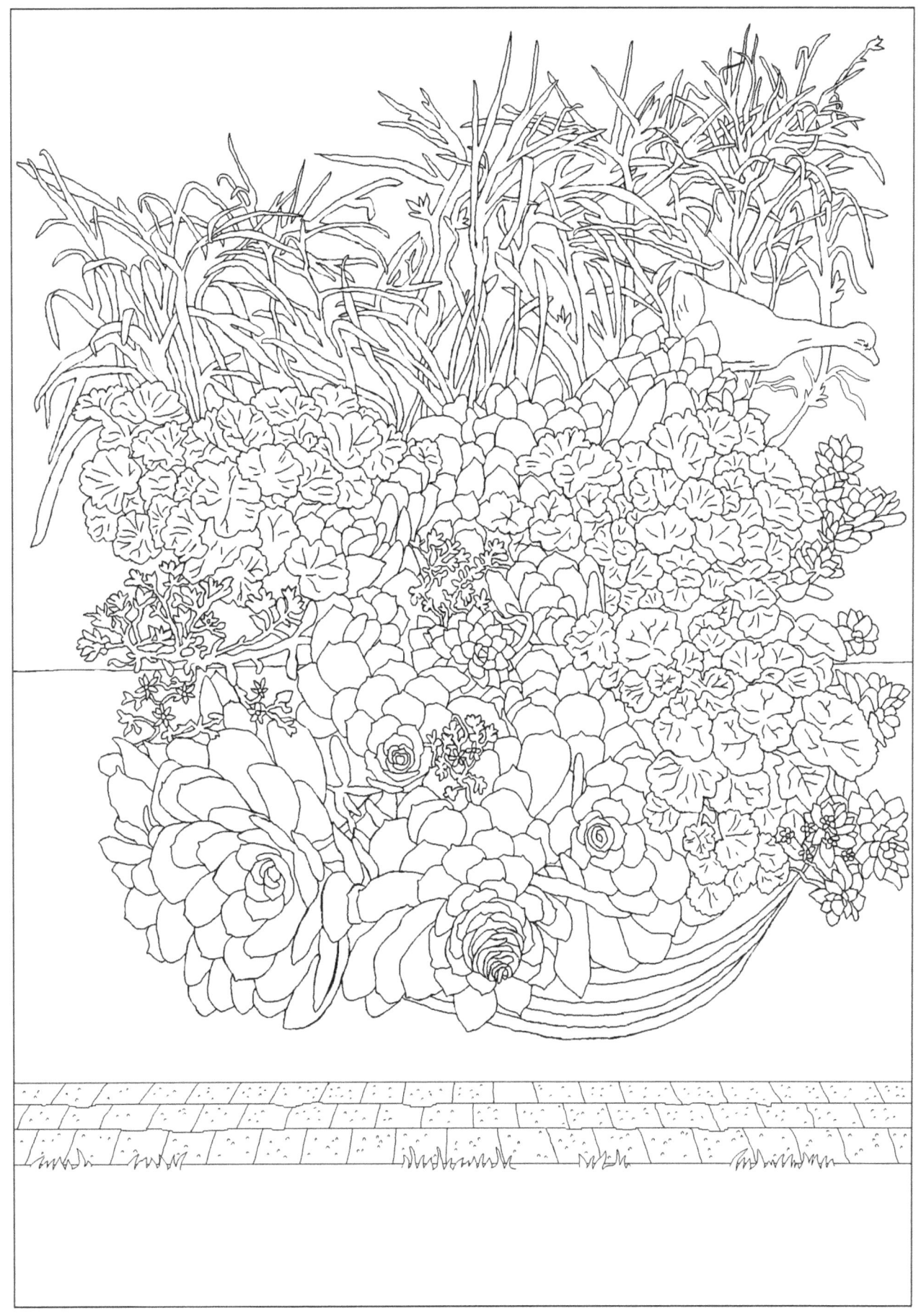

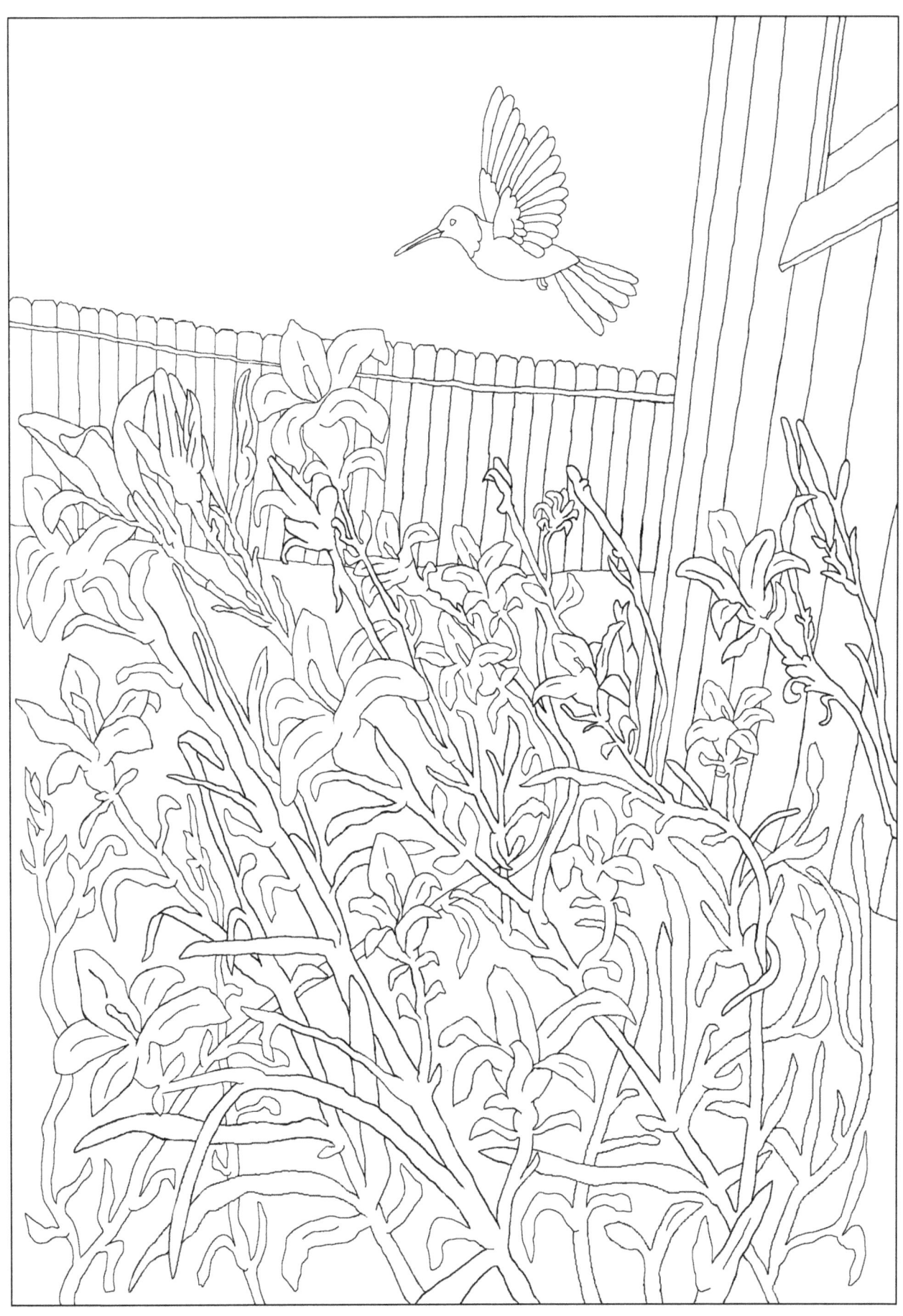

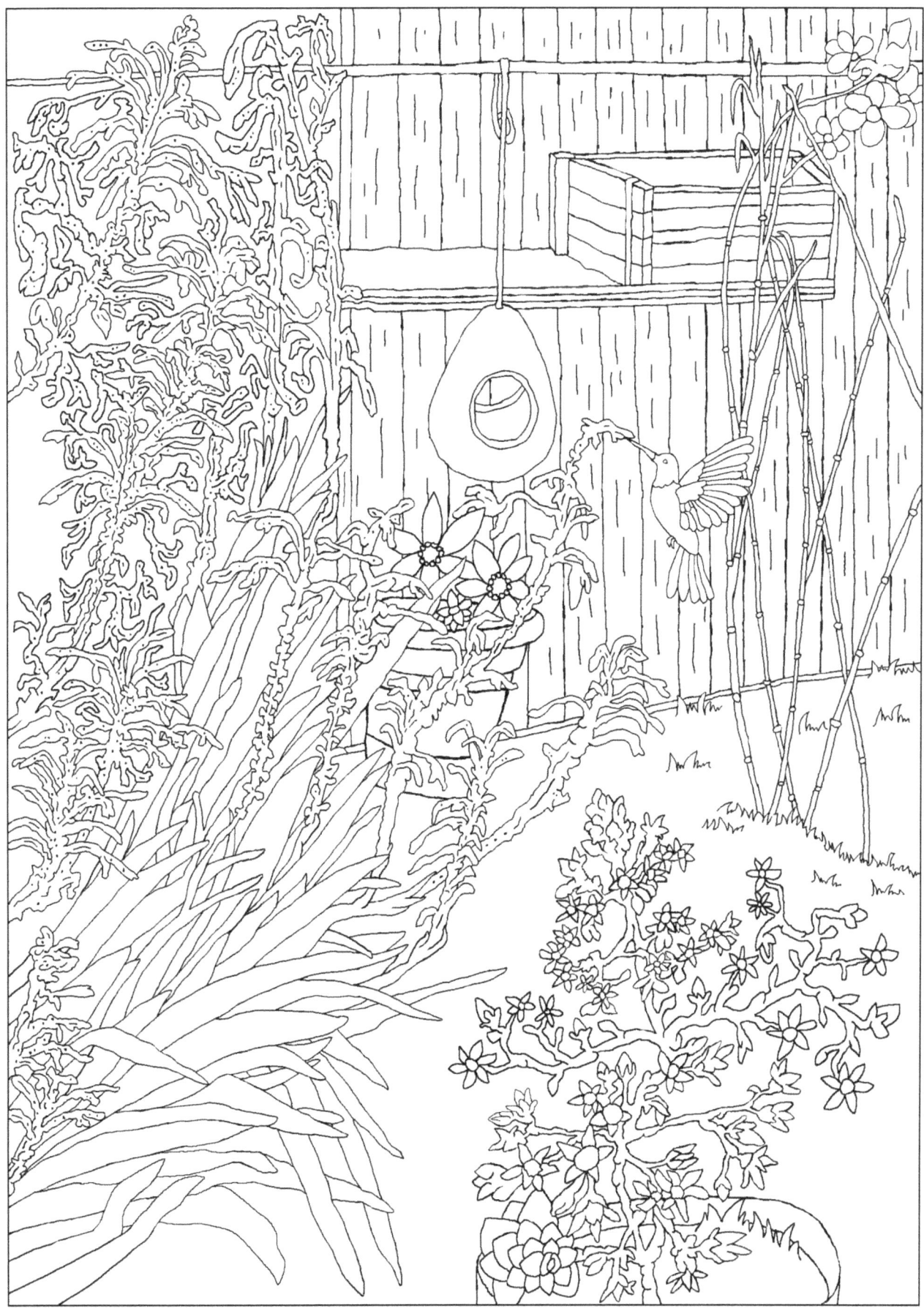

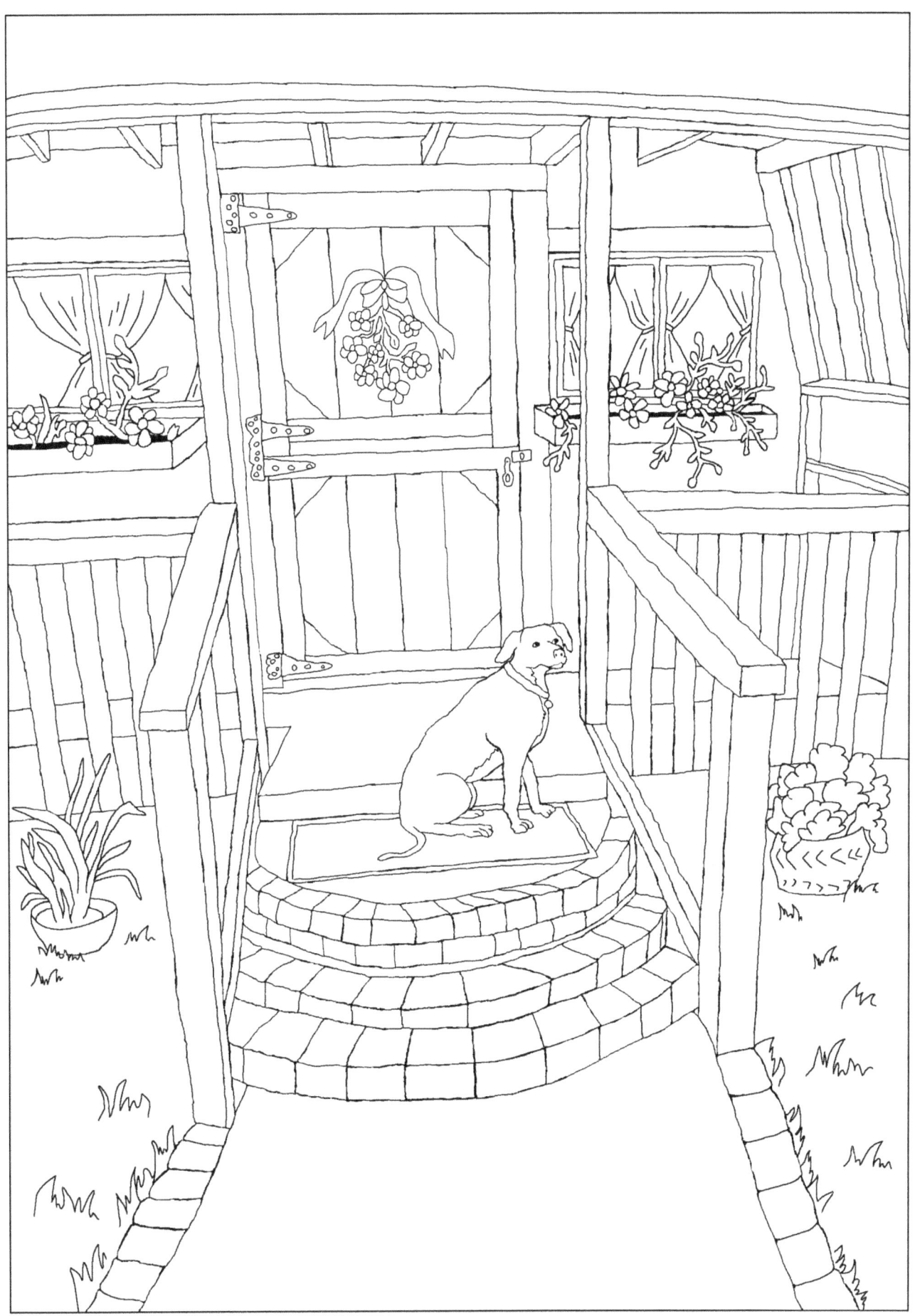

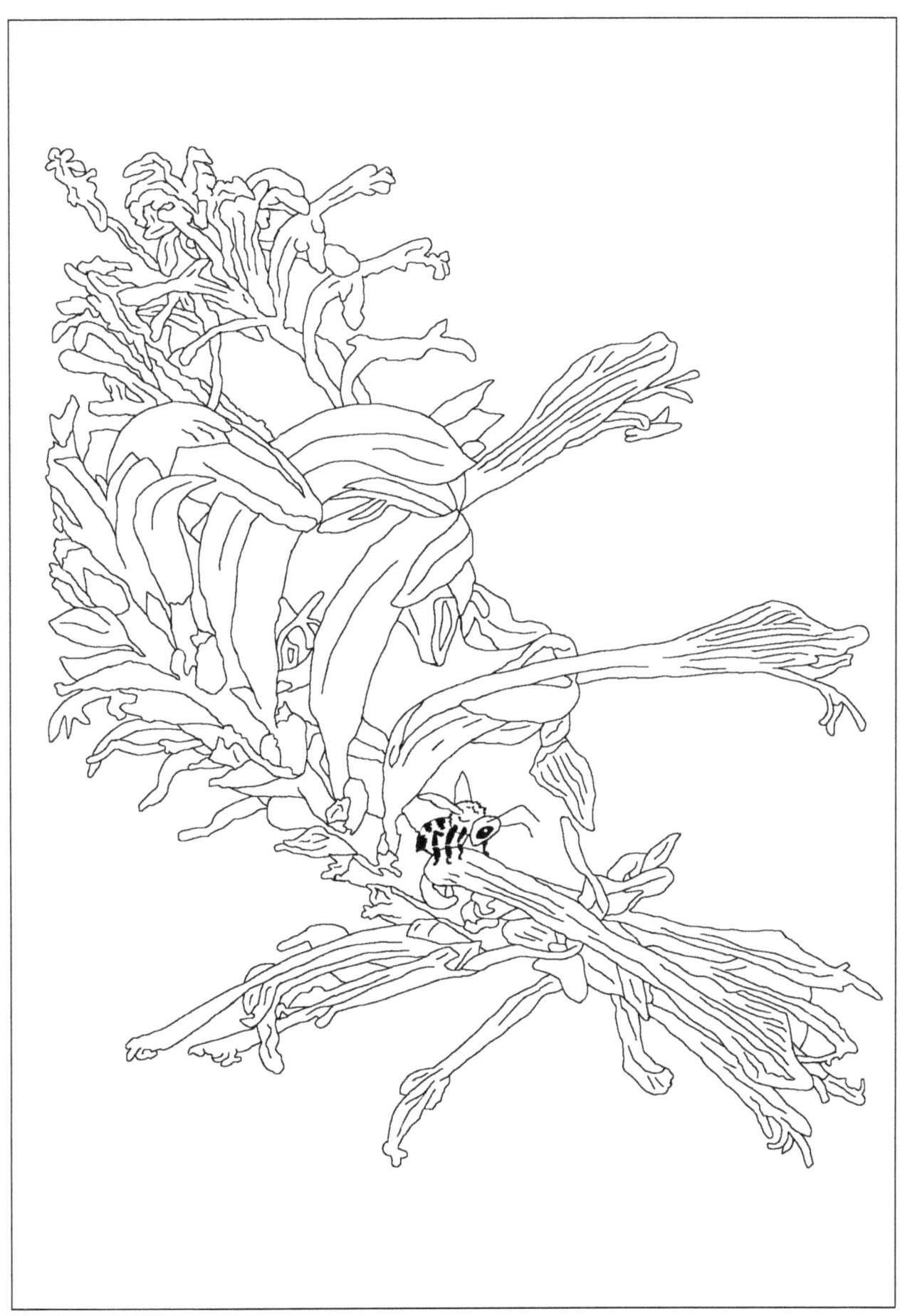

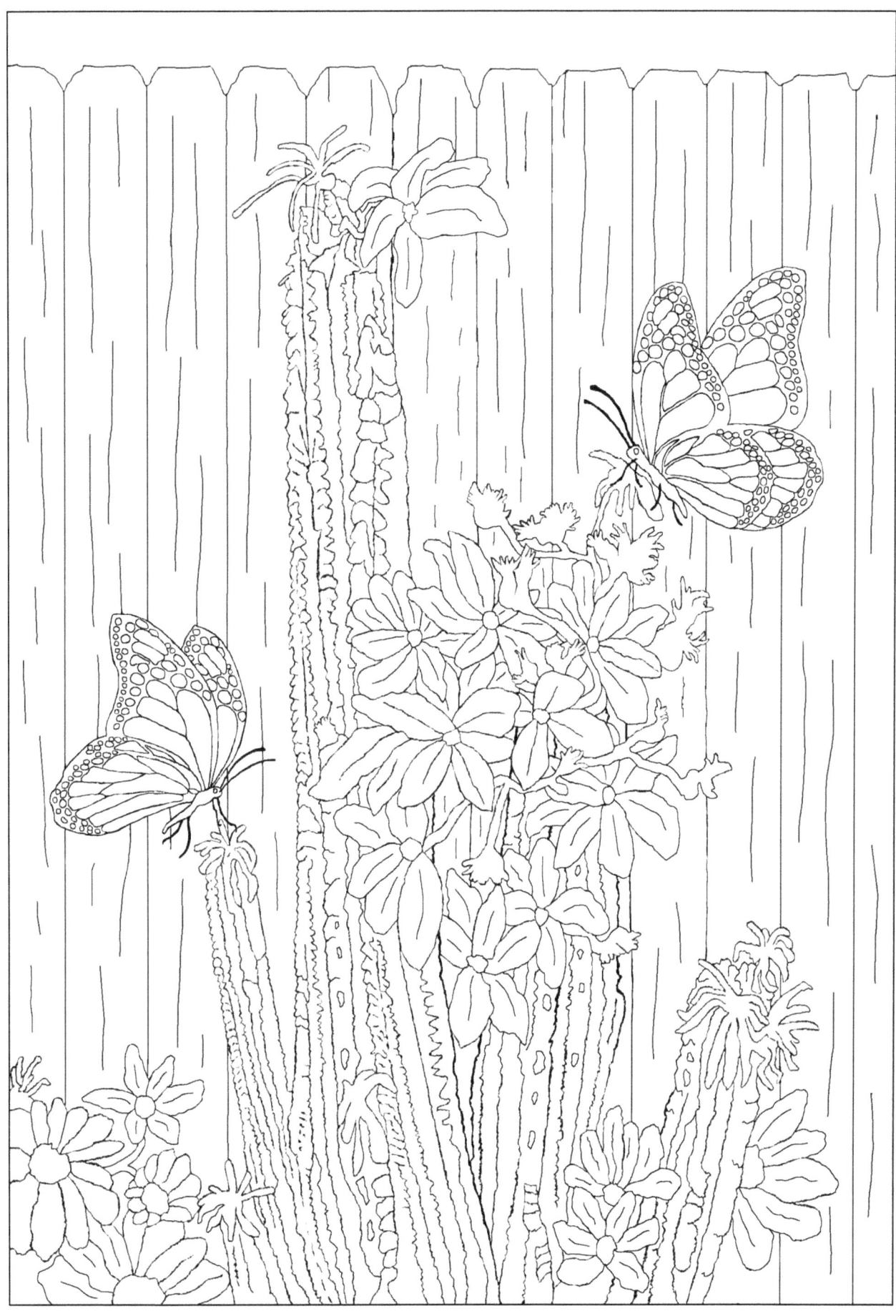

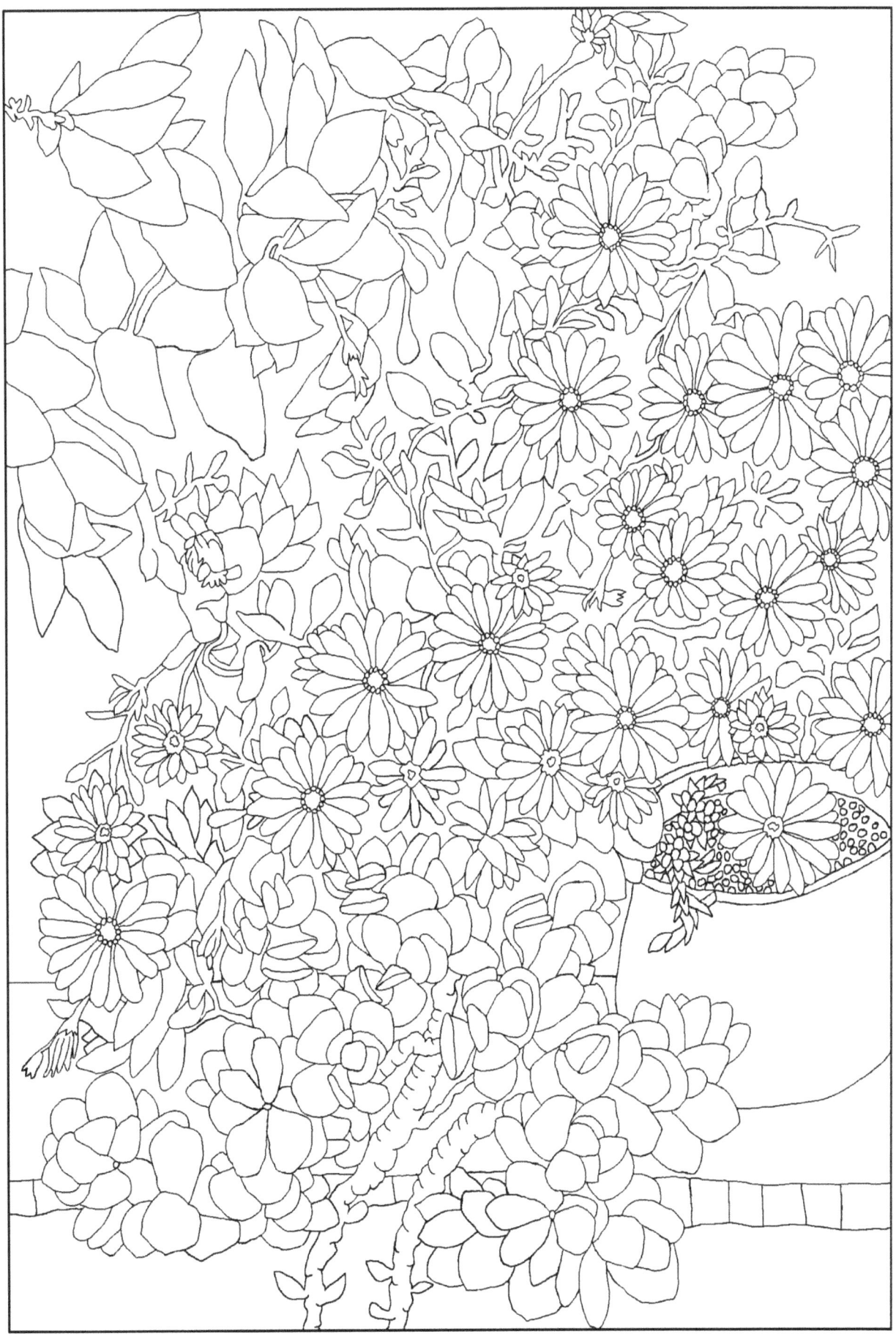

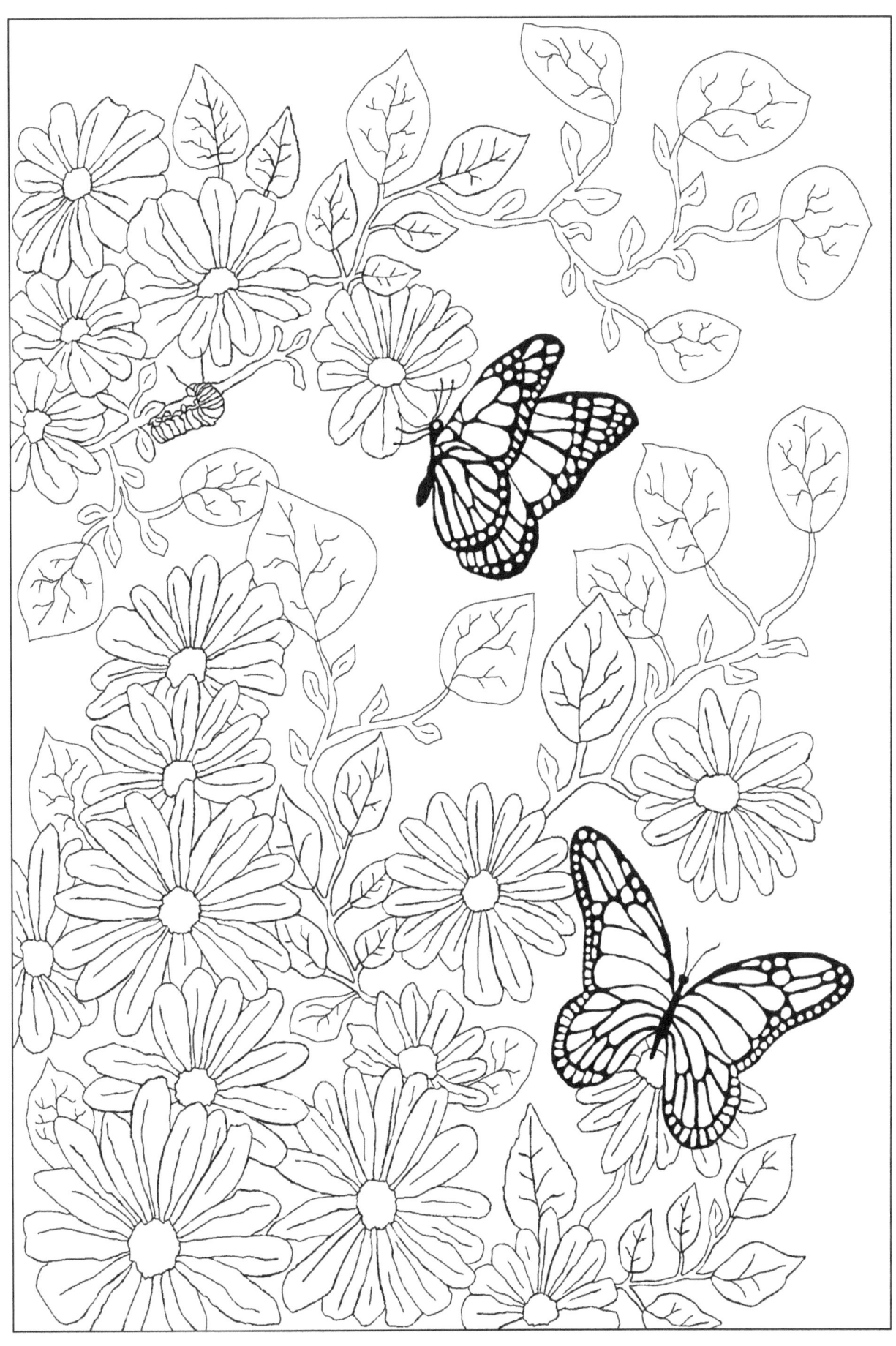

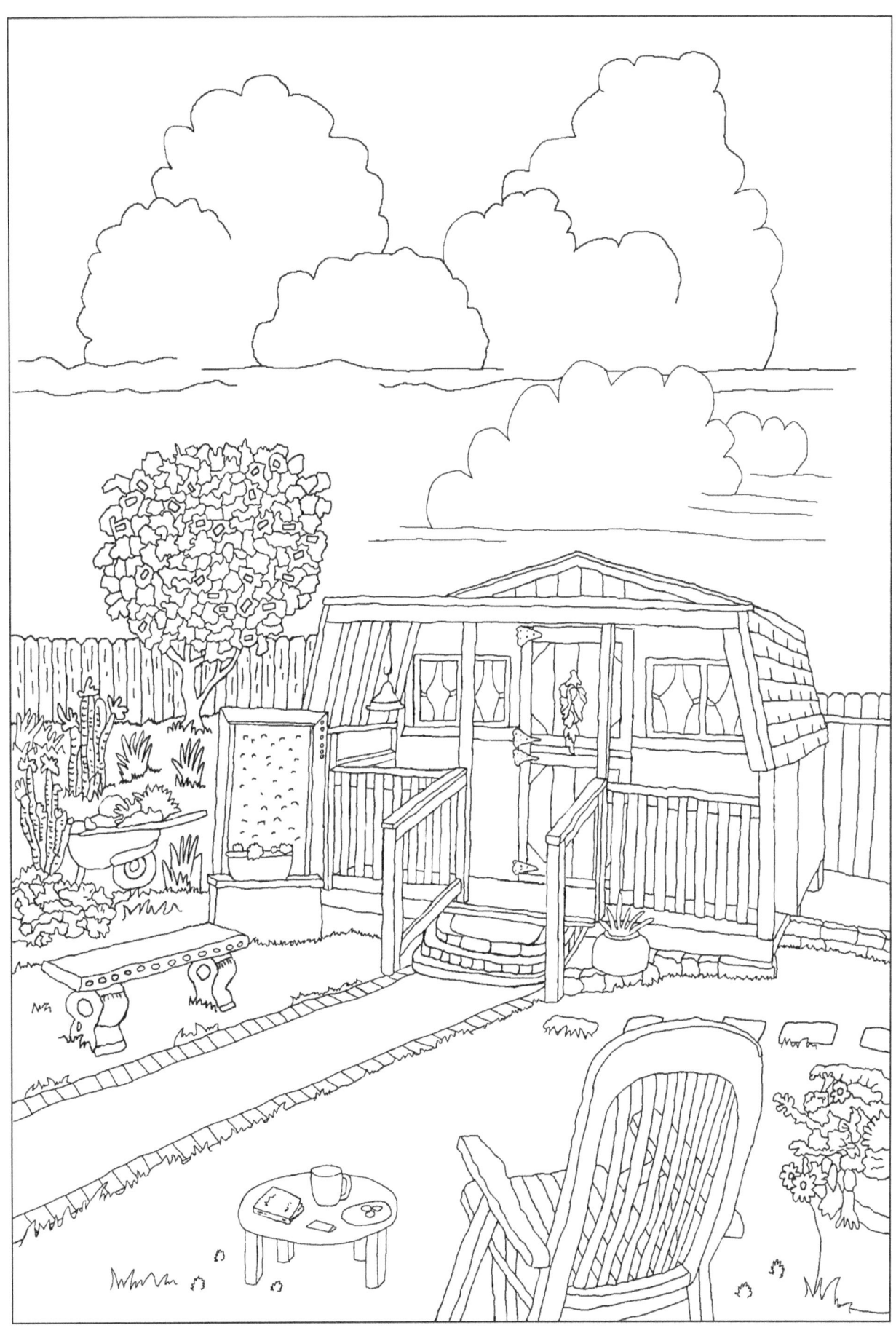

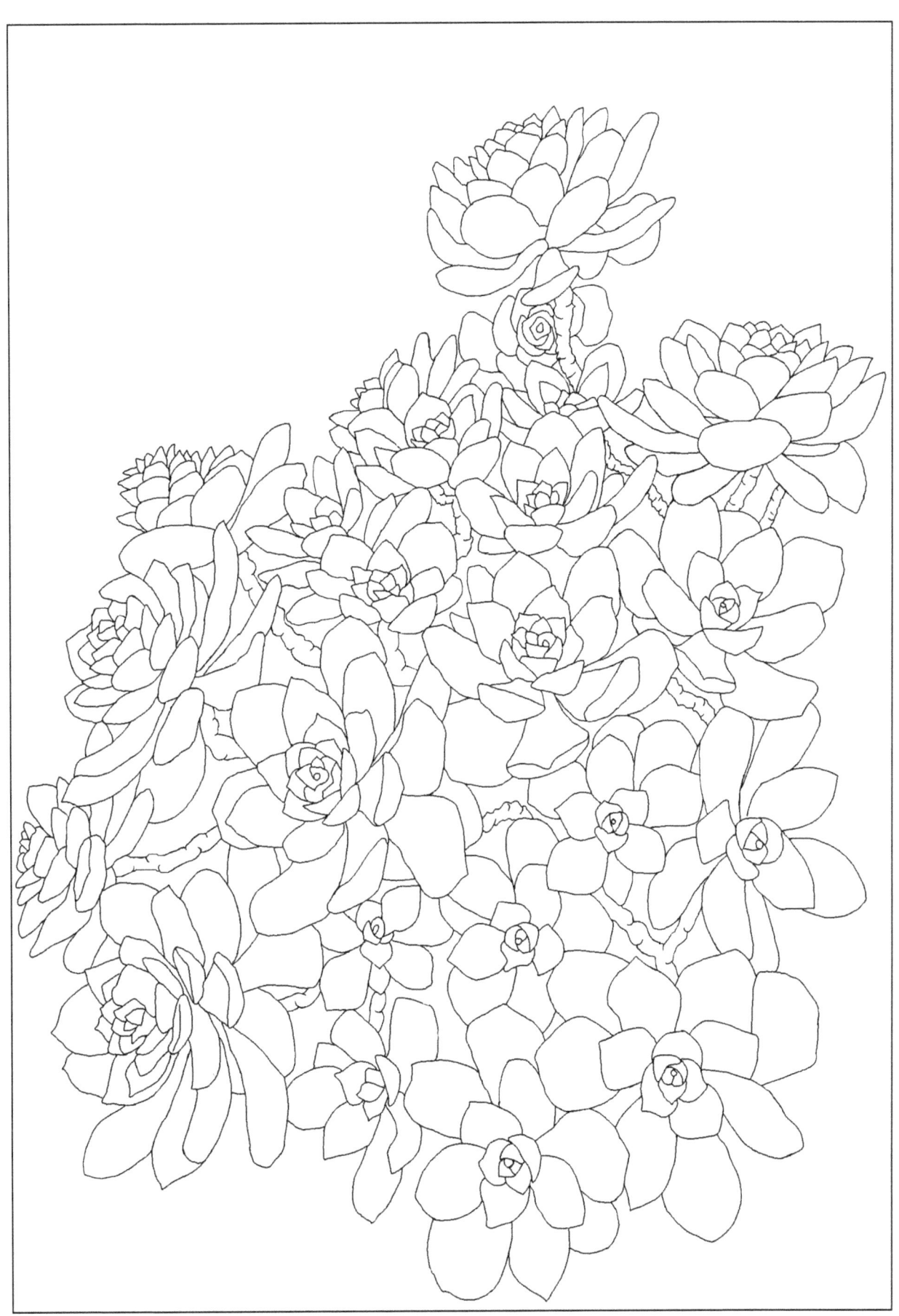

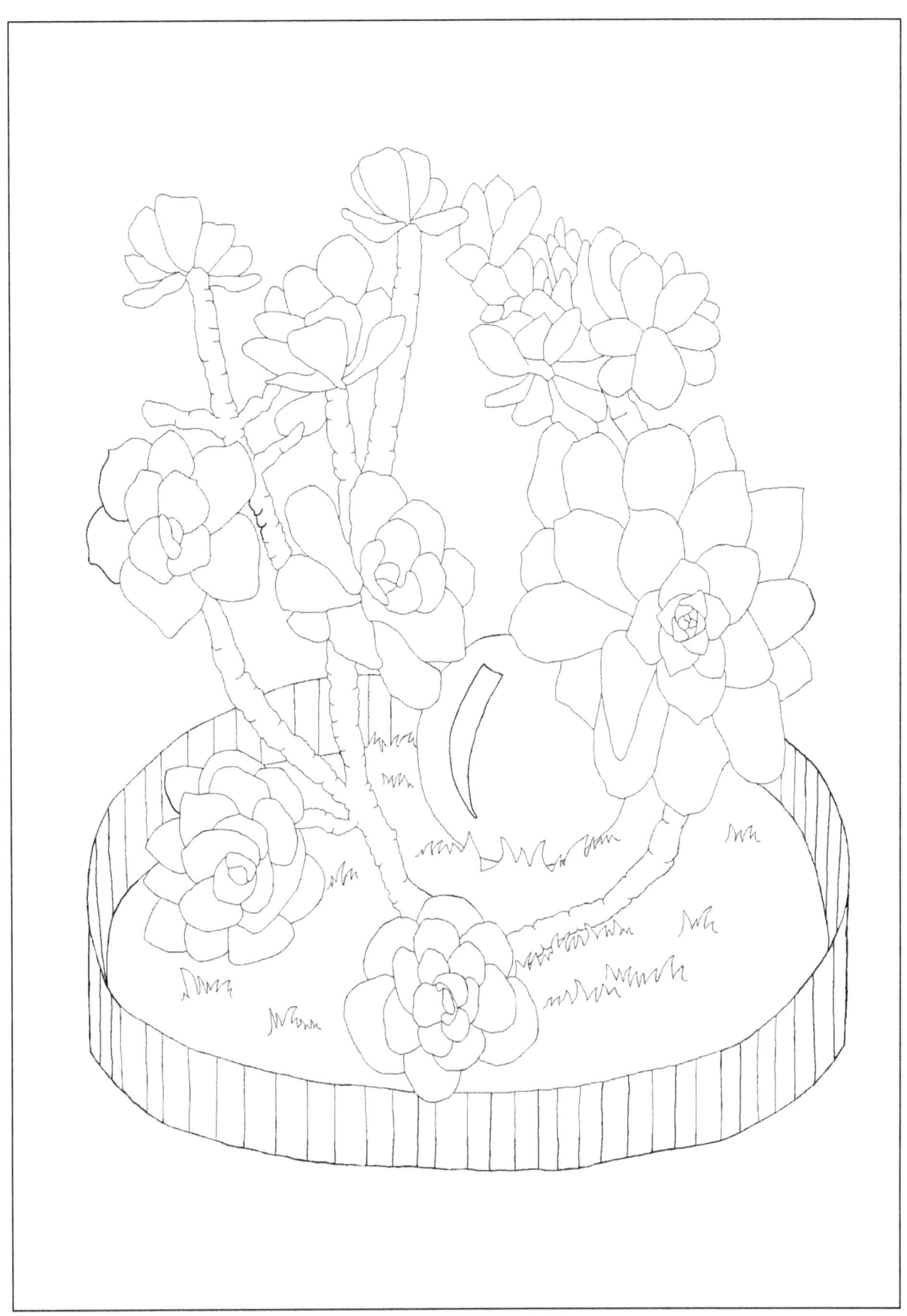

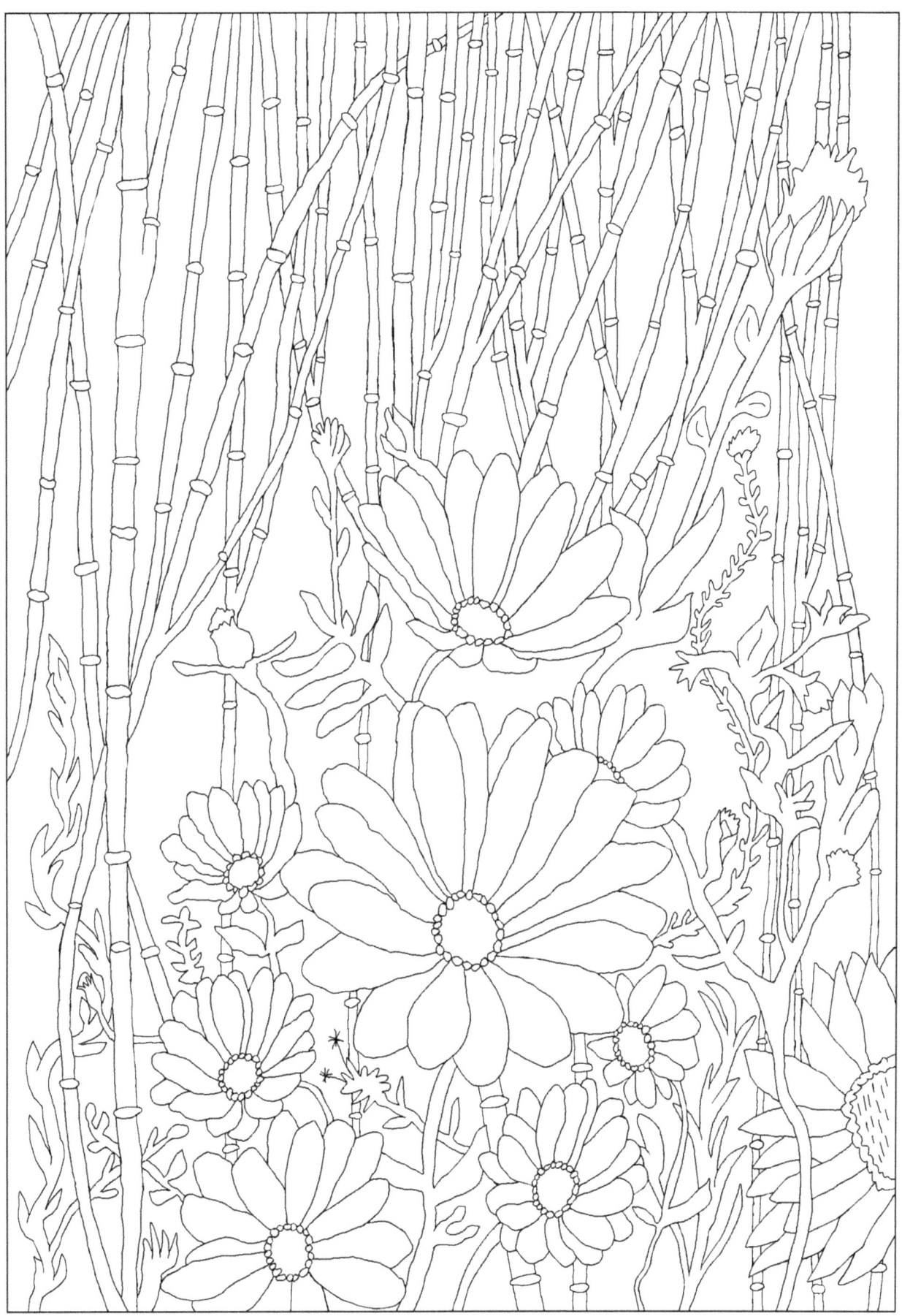

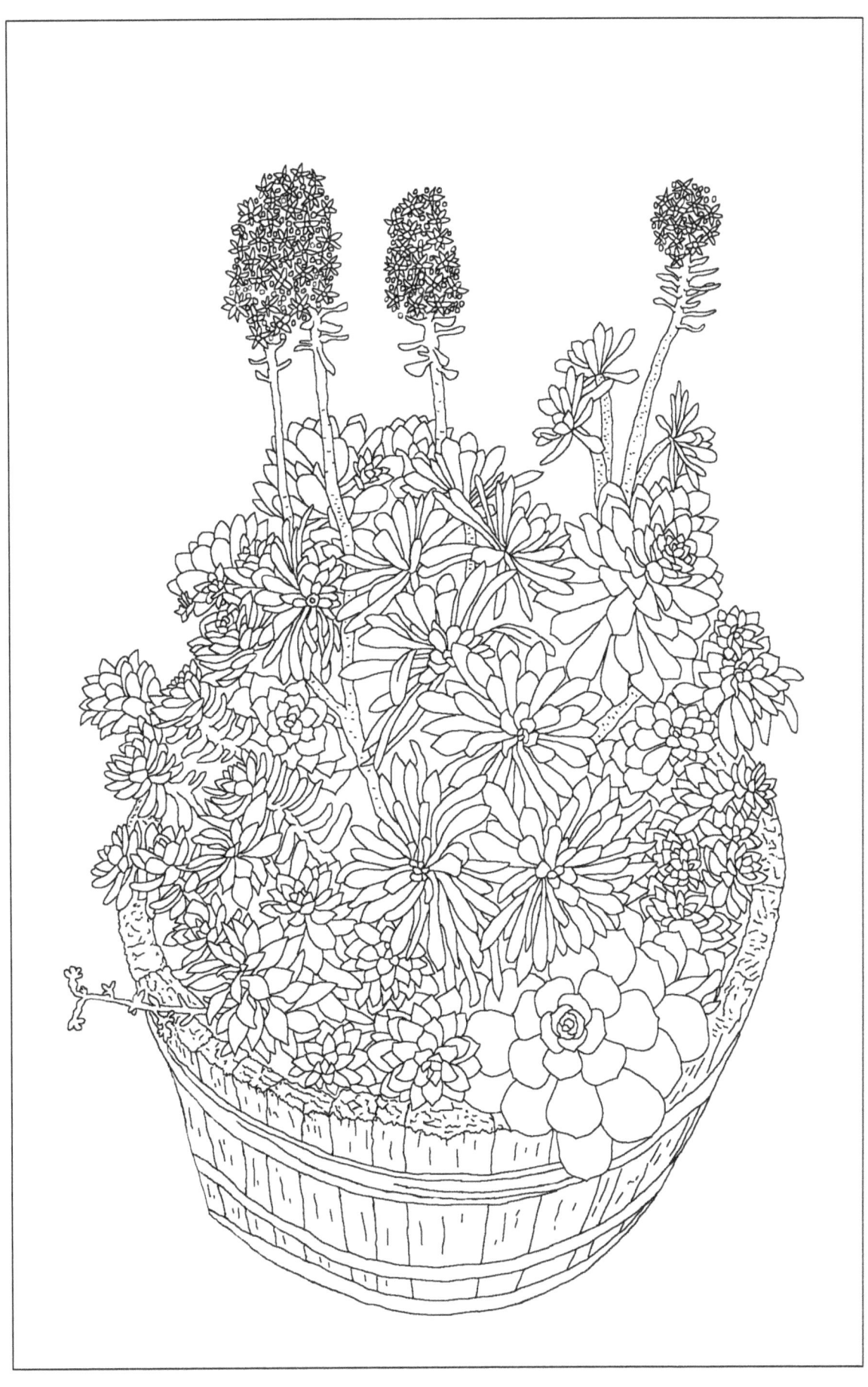

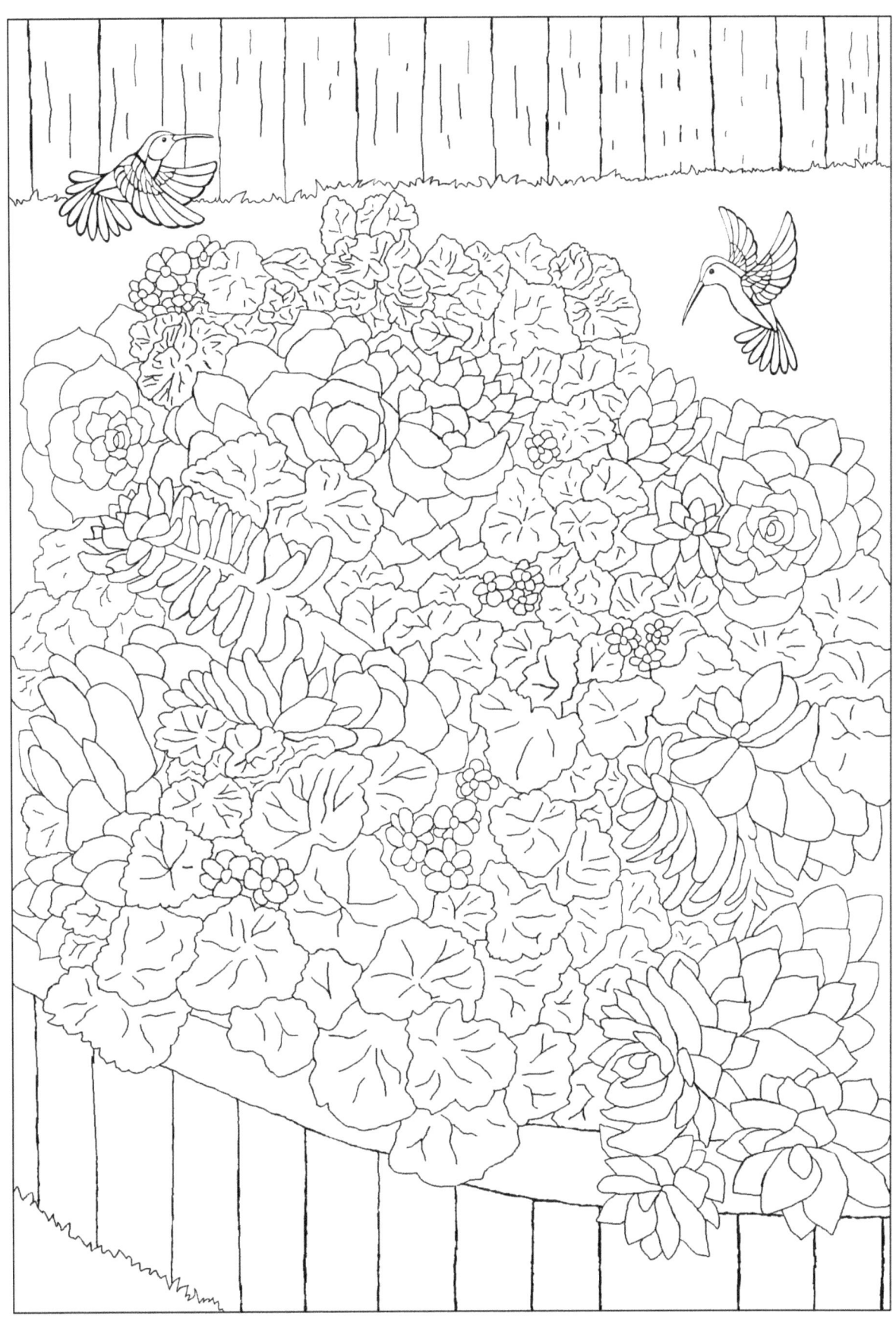

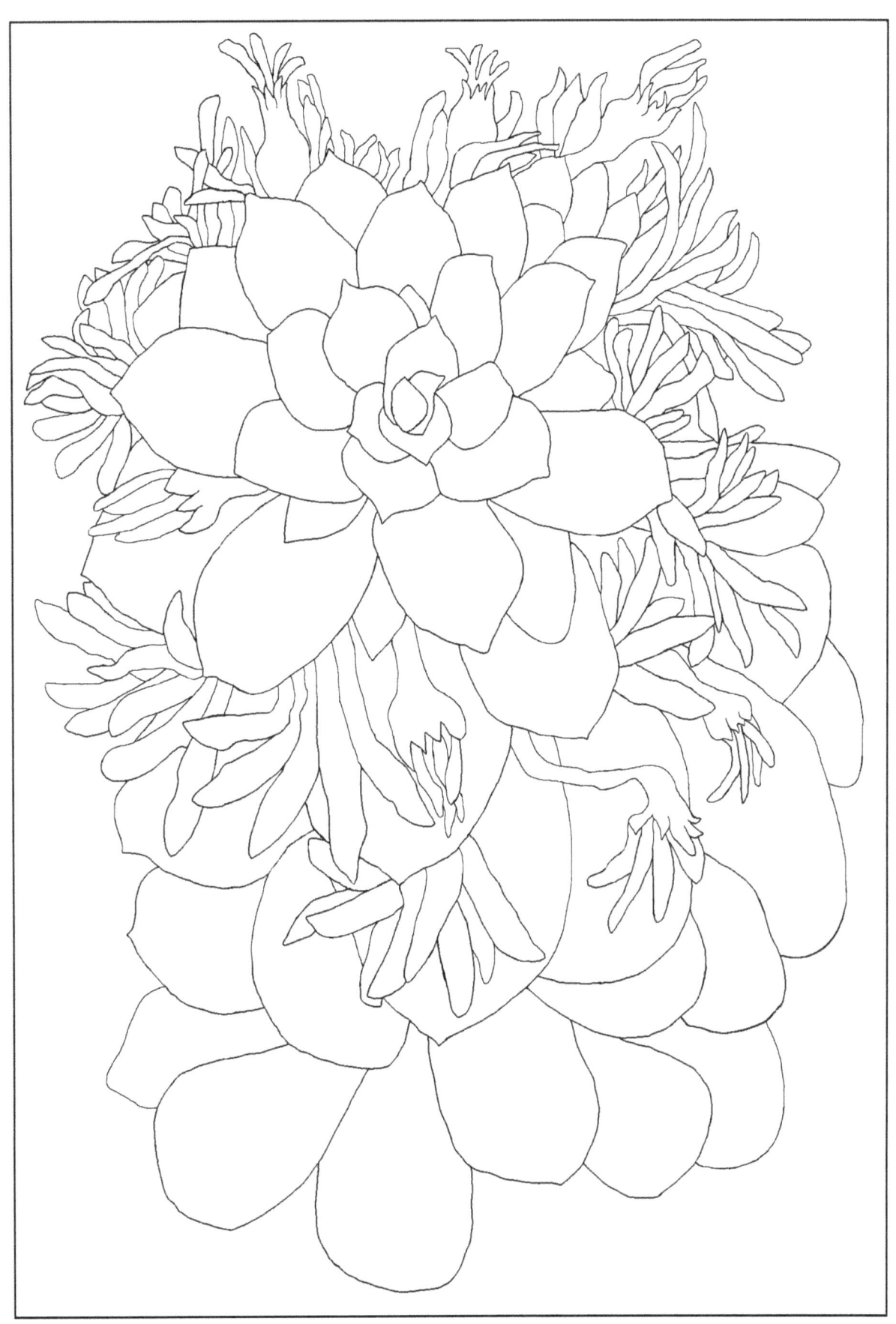

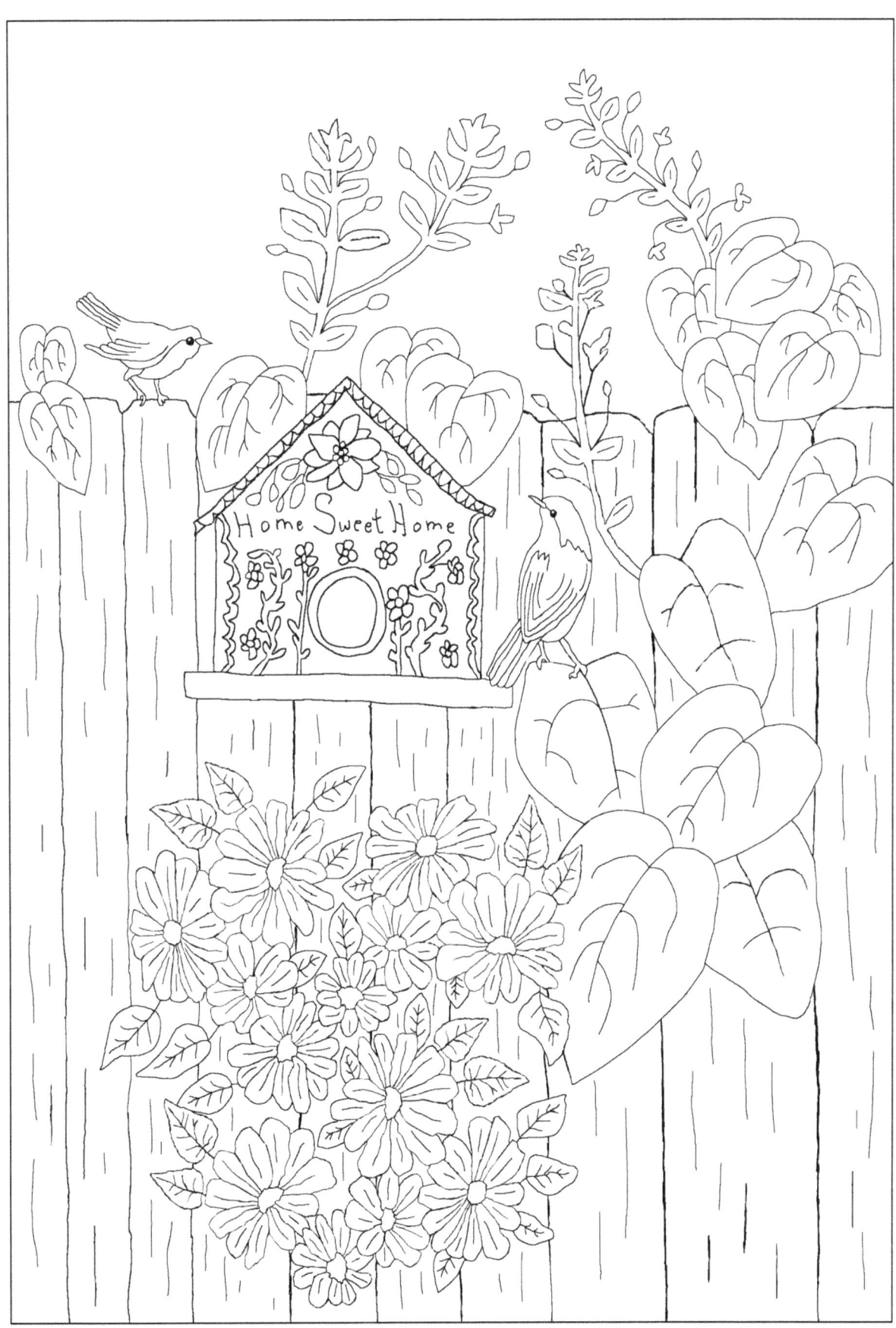

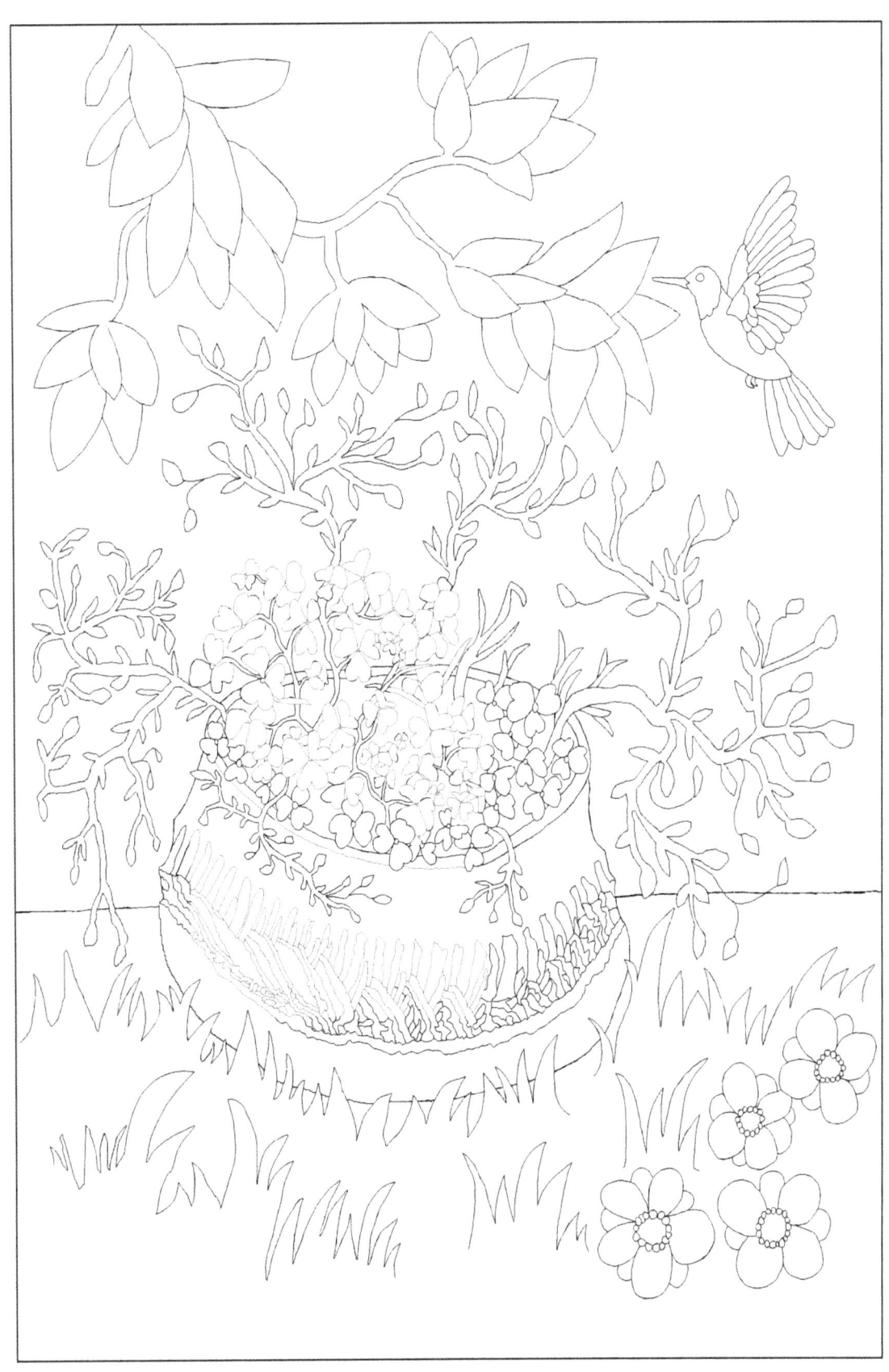

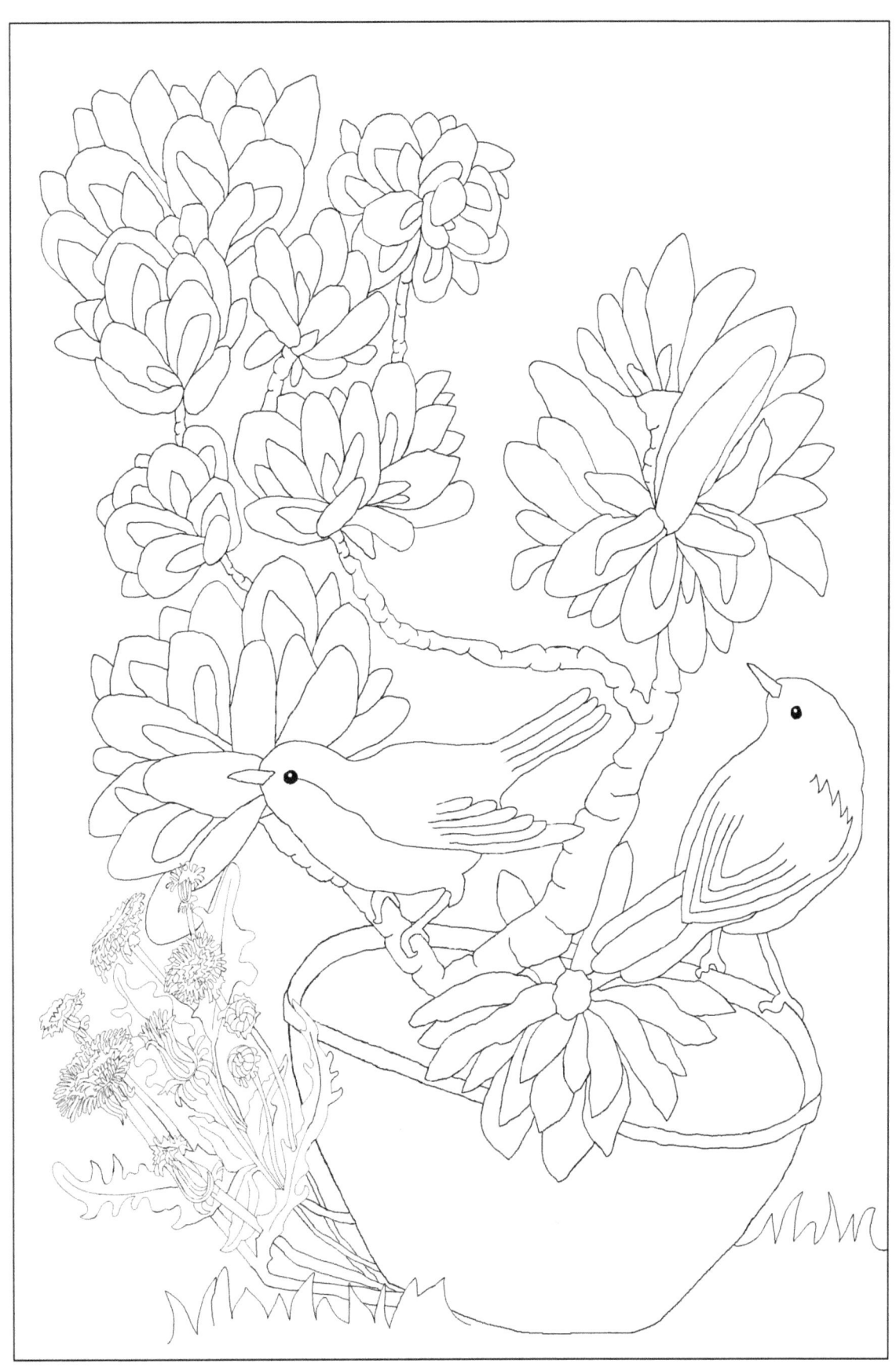

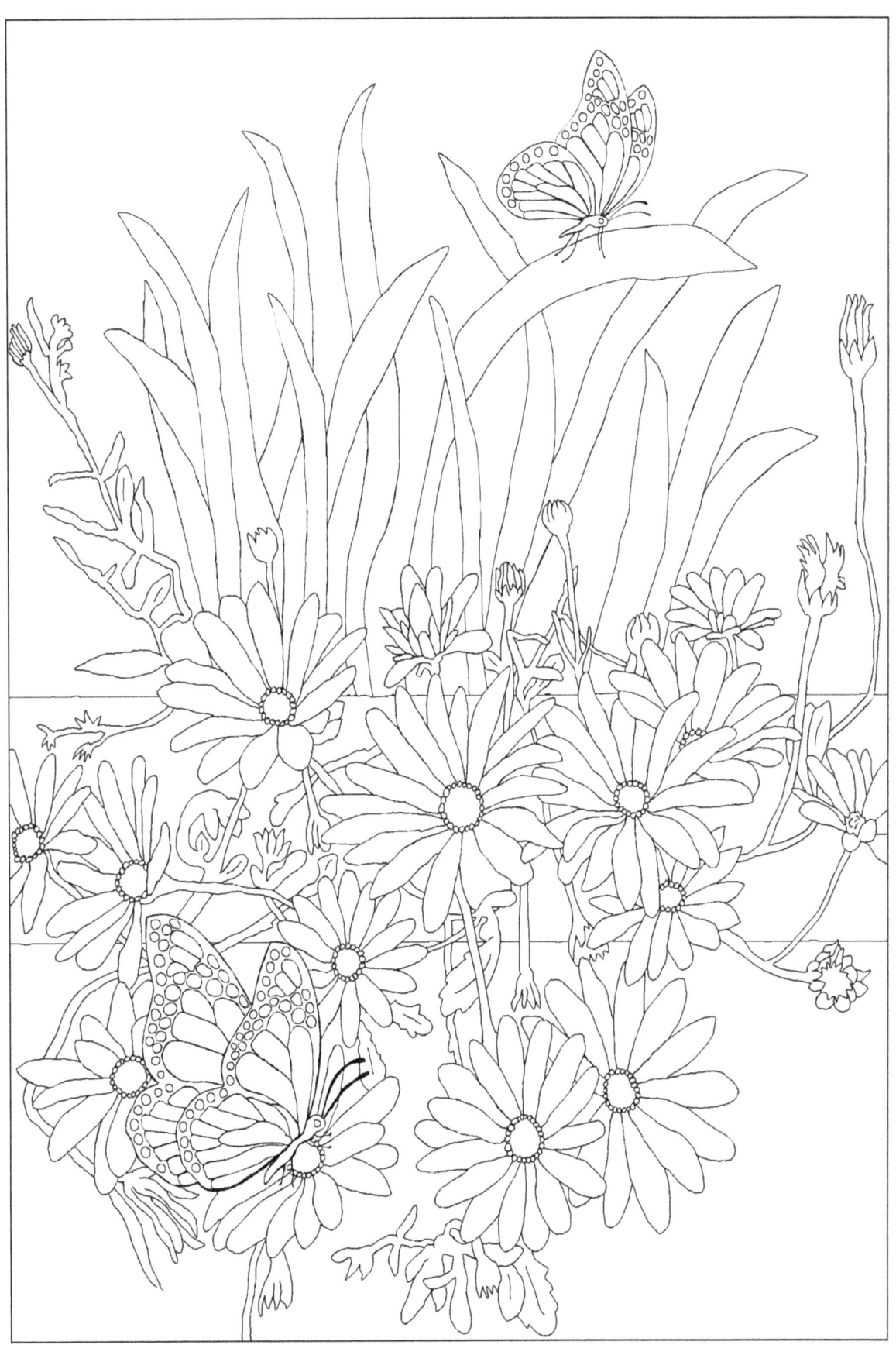